A Velvet Increase of Curiosity

A VELVET INCREASE OF CURIOSITY

Lise Downe

ECW PRESS

Some of these poems/earlier versions have surfaced in *Avec*, *Writing*, *screens and tasted parallels*, *Raddle Moon*, and *West Coast Line*.

Thanks to: Karen MacCormack for her ongoing support, and to the many others who have provided encouragement; also to the Explorations Program of The Canada Council and the Writers' Reserve Program of the Ontario Arts Council for their generous assistance; and to Bruce Whiteman for guiding this book into print.

Canadian Cataloguing in Publication Data

Downe, Lise
A velvet increase of curiosity

Poems.

ISBN 1-55022-199-X

I. Title
PS8557.087V35 1993 C811'.54 C93-094244-2
PR9199.3.D78V35 1993

The general editor of ECW poetry books is Bruce Whiteman.

Published with the assistance of The Canada Council and the Ontario Arts Council.

Cover design by Lise Downe and Gordon Robertson.
Photograph by Thomas Fricke.
Set in Stempel Garamond and Trajan types
by ECW Type & Art, Oakville, Ontario.

Distributed by General Distribution Services,
30 Lesmill Road, Toronto, Ontario M3B 2T6.

Published by ECW PRESS,
1980 Queen Street East, Toronto, Ontario M4L 1J2.

MASTER: "John, where did you learn to sing like that?"

SLAVE: "I'm not singin', suh. I'm jus' hollerin' to help me with livin' " . . .

Quote from the back of the album: A Christian Testimonial *by The Dixie Hummingbirds (Peacock Records).*

CONTENTS

Scorched 9
Predestined In Twelve Parts 13

First Blush

Intuition 27
Cloudburst 28
Summertime Brochure 29
To Think Of As Here 30
Confused And Future Assemble 31
Limbless 32
We race to drill 34
A Gigantic Quiet 35
Equal Grace 36
Shift 38

Whole Sailing

Greeting The Downpour 47
It breaks down 48
Not Hear . . . Yet 49
Articulation 50
And Shine Alike 51
Residue Thc Probe 52
Showing The Whites 53
Hence My Pallor 54
Depth Of Field 55
In Her Errant Verity 56
Style 59

Abundance Of Shores 60
Invention Of Early Afternoon 61
Awakening 62
Soft Ground And Telescopic 63
Vehicle 64
Witness 65
Dextrous Crawl 66
So To Speak 67

Scorched

A distant calm inhales, drawing up
across the deserted clearing.
Smoldering remains of artifice.
And I am conscious
not of fear,
but of a terrible exultation.
Motion.   Less.

One geography of shapes remembered.
      Given.
Mind describes a thread of smoke.
Shifting thought.   Burning sand.
For everything has climbed
the inner threshold a spectrum
I almost see through.
Perfectly.   White.

Lime tree laden with thirst.
But never what I expected.

Predestined In Twelve Parts

Inside the vestibule flooded with sunshine
inflaming a blouse amid many freckles.
Your ankles searching no less than.
A few fragments through amber dust
lie the desolation of a long coat
and hammocks.

Pray for me a rarer pink and white awakening.
Eastward
northward
one part still   scattered   stirred
informed with curious   almost humorous
intonation.
Sheet of words shimmering diffuse a glow.
    In time the wide brim.

One is influenced   more or less
seized   concluded   returned.
One is influenced.
The mouth finds a letter
silver harness the lantern
in gold mosaics
her furnace.
Myself.
Burned vast walls the primitive dialect
ruins to temples these forests freestone.

2.

Not long afterward
some little time
so long
finally
at once.
Mauve marble her heels between two steps
in recollected divinity.
Distant summits azure melting
stream gigantic.
The narrow road descent.

For this in blue they served a hedge of scarlet.
Velvet came smiling to make him think
the texture of habit a subtle richness.

To escape.   To stay.
To ride on alone the nearer distance.

3.

In the hush of a calm blind front
a flash of yellow
smothered south and gentle slope
flat-roofed.
Arched.
Sheltered heraldic cunning.

The mast
from time to water that plunge
swallowtail exiles a nascent dignity.
Cavernous stairways rumble.

The keyhole confines a new thought.
Churches perish a perversity intones.

4.

Bare feet pervade that dim chamber.
Costume a doubt of identity
features unfold pantomime.

The path cultivated by necessity after a time
long ribbon of cloud.
Words break from her wet and cold.
The slightest sound expands.

5.

Truth told.   A thief.
And the ring slipped off.
She   was afraid.
Between walls of green
finding a trail through this labyrinth
all the branches swaying inside their house
turned pale with a passionate gesture.
Even the roof   the narrow doorway   into corners
the floor was the answer and smooth again.

Where a careless step would rouse the echo
of this spot.
Mingled refuse and wildflower.
Their shadows lay cold on the high wall
violent in outline but touched here and there.
Uneven rows through the gloom.
The west had faded.

All the world invisible
the gleam of many torches clustered   reared
and staggered on.
The story of her loss broadcast
from its long sleep
struggling.

An unearthly wail.

Silencc.

He could not have heard her.
Isolated
yet shining.

6.

Set down the candle
storm clouds another life
culminate and hover thick above her head.
Something repeating in a strange primordial.
Some thing repeating.

> It's a different point-of-view
> from another viewpoint.

Into slavery extravagant and empty
wilderness bends
the truth of your eyes and mine.
She realized
she saw
she felt an eternity.

> The wind had changed.
> Hope flickered.

Sweet lemon thunderous impotence.
Silver foliage over marigold.
Worth
while in life.

7.

In the rocky clearing approach lay motionless.
Image of a hand   index and the fragment
wrapped in yellow mist
trembling before her.

She would go on living this hour
an inarticulate glance.
Calm and motion less blinding
binding the tangled flowers.

8.

Crevices wedged at intervals entwined or blushed.
Links that hold soil and fray.
Hunting in the woods of his words
it hardly matters.
Red blooms again even rarer than before.

Let fall the thorn.
Deep blue satin then purple twilight.

A few steps to and fro   the woman
something he imagined
her   to be.
His mirror a non-reflective surface.

9.

Just as vast   countless
say there was nothing.
By comparison far too much.
One instead of many vertebrae
the few little figures afloat between
fading sooner
than expected.

Terrain trains the mind's recognition of its own
surroundings.
She found
                        herself again.
Stained glass rosettes roll in howling
with faith.

10.

Three bottles excited by a fringe of trees.
Emerald   sapphire   and ruby.
      Two birds.
      One stone.

A broken stool more impossible
but with a sort of splintered exasperation.
You must be
what might ever have been
first intentions.
More air.

Taste the tongue
pure body a swift crossing.
Disorder a momentary bafflement
never before imagined.
Every fiber a vague premonition rising
toward different ends.

For an atheist?
The certainty of something.

11.

Through the woods the sky from navy to gold
perception her nature contemplates.
    The old life up there.
Fish make me climb this hill
extenuation their secrets a surmise of mine.
Water and steel before the church door
take root and bear the miraculous.

Sanctuary tender that drum.

12.

Fortune in time sees another
moment.
It seems to me.
Who laughed now the spirit that followed within
the process.
Hands from pockets.   Windows open.
Fingers immense through darkness
embrace another world.

Touch the earth   horizon the same distance
intimate and then the light.
Beautiful by turns
silence curves a painted eye.

    The moon is up.

Drawing close to me   the very point of changing
through everything unchanged.

A clearing
into the heart.

FIRST BLUSH

Intuition

into the whole
our lives
a definite size
something other than ourselves
      it doesn't matter what it is

the various feelings
in so many syllables
a sort of tension
in relation to what can happen

suddenly a curiosity
of small spaces
the dictionary compelled to write a poem
      freely
and which you can read
      freely

eyes to ears   nose to mouth

repeating the words
      utterly   utterly
the sniff that follows
various shades of green

Cloudburst

upper circles drawn to the heavenly
host through thought
motion like water whispers
fruitful   frightful connection

perhaps more than formless to lack
of form
good faith as biological
ambition dissolving to insight
the world but the world not
story
            issue
and the rain choirs

Summertime Brochure

Intending to stay
they sat in blue morning glory
all hours coming into the room.
Being one another could almost touch
past a wall
urging alchemy in the face of a chosen future.
Years of night attend this early eloquence
forgetting the moment a humming silence.

Released with half-smile in a great big glass.
Pale golden.   Sparkling.
Sweet monotone around and around
echo the centre her own voice
her own imagination over the bannister
circulating once again through the body of the world.

A century after
fugitive and evanescent
that remedy tasted stairwell
perhaps or the tropics.

To Think Of As Here

Typical of square afternoons leaning with conscious pleasure.   Milled about   exactly reversal through errand. Bringing them back   interior like a sponge washed up after a meal to gather and sunset his blue-veined hand.   Blew hot and cold.   Move back the table forever furniture   scrape brow and cheek.   Cozy nuance an armchair beside the road. Truth a characteristic jerk.

Postures migrate a radical of meaning   function connotation this chapter in prose.   Stigmata in situ.

Attendant.   Cradle.   Forth.

pressed a hand not to mention a little shocking.
Tempt us.   Withold the news and tell everyone.   Up-rooted
and white lilac you are here covered with trellises.   Too
lazy to lift a finger and stammering description to shift
content.   Unnoticed or unknown everything has run its course.
Plain to a solved riddle.
Gravel paths reluctant intuition   a knocking to seek it
elsewhere and find it here.   Write it all down having glimpsed
some remarkable. Thought heard through deafness thought desire
in vain.   Lighter or darker repeated more or less.
Instil us a queer cocoon.

Limbless

Limbless through held water
withered rushes
unequaled splendour in a single year.
Lake and tower.   Terraces.
Rushing down to a still higher
auspicious rain.

I have heard the calyx again
every sign afresh through the wide infinity
    grains and drops
day and night fall from the sky.

There is no end side by side.
Do not ask me   this lamp the ferry
and the stone overhead
circumference at the centre.
Flicker of eyelid dreams
shape and dissolve.
Felt hand a smile to radiant joy.

*

In pictorial script the fluid form
granted not with words.
I can only describe its effect:

"Once upon a time, there lived
quiet as grass and shrub
a spirit of the river.
He merited my grace.
Whose throat and arm displayed
interlacing rafters.
A vague splendour one could come round to.
Like scent of azalea.

Then the merciless glow
swelled and rippled.
Friction a whirling tumult sweet and pure.
Current heavy in the roaring.
Night invaded a small room making
little eddies and pockets.
      Adrift
the sound of breathing over
infinite ocean.
Exquisite refuge in darkness.
Fugitive hint of nutmeg
his guiding fingers grinning reconciled.

When the room had been swept circular
movement beyond the pond repeated itself.
      Over and over.
Rubbed off flushing the rising sun."

We race to drill the largest holes.
The boat's main purpose is buoyancy.

The idea of the boat
is to drill a common drift in us.

A Gigantic Quiet

The sphere rolls real and grazed
compelled in all its glory.
Stories come down to this spot
pronounced by a wrist
                              twisting and turning.
We could say the words fit the sloping
path
spiralling down every time
I carry them this way.
Destined for the predestined.
A bargain in mind.
      Enshrined.

Solstice in shrubbery
I have described olive
                                        wax   and
young?   Man?

Mangled in
the press remains cerulean.
Urn and promise
re-assembling gut and bone
to ether
                or

Equal Grace

Carving this massive frame
chestnut on the periphery
golden curls fall to the brightest blue floor.
A sigh of regret.   Buttermilk.
Familiarity gathered with ease
borrowing difference to straighten.
Wind-swept viridian
almost level the ringing nature of a bell.

An article
a ripple is honey waxed.
Liquid a mouthful to goodness.
So much lost in order to be found.
Countless reels of celluloid grove
and scatter
upon entering what happens to women
like me.

What's in a name?
No reason   but
to get word back ward
some grammatical cistern running through.
"Good morning!" nearly bumping into the dawn.

    And how do I awaken?

A combination of thrilled and pacified
rustling full sail spellbound porpoise.
Thirsty! to kiss evening on edge
and weaving thought turned by a nod.

Night of nights.
Pure form to fill it.
Dread infinite steady
in the wild wood.

Shift

It was beyond a little east
so brightly moonlight of blossom.
This shadow offering evergreen
between leaf and needle
the hollow lowing mossy with crocus.
Spicy and moist exultation.
Meridian red star toward the west
toward the west only further south
fugitive rays a tall flame.
There were eyes here.
Twilight they smiled upon broken step
all round pail and dipper.
Silver lifting soft dialogue
ancestor to express from lungs
the open question.

2.

Spring a new station
smoothing but a mild reflection
the early rains.
Lukewarm darkness and the clarity
for thirst.
Down to the little to drink.
This is the tale in person
in a group of trees
from what heaven or cloud was entangled
then released
bow and quivering.

It is here to tell of
the seed with other events.
The beginning and not the end.
For spirit safeties an elegant drone
warm and whatsoever
with peacock
feathers.

3.

If one speaks of retaining the flavour
as “sporting” the dim and wise
only now and again craved
for eating by the blazing fire.
One lies softer.
Strengthened in monosyllables
before the complicated nature of the whole.
Not so easily answered.
The balance a larger
and more significant footstep
walking damp and expectant
when the hour is come.

I know not the day.
I know not which or shall
the field with seeing hands
to all within.

4.

A great errand of cedar and sycamore.
Filigree through the text
a natural hollow for refuge
and look-out.
This road so differently placed.

The well articulates gold and opal
embroidered with laughter.
A hole well-lined and known to throw
itself broad as daylight
into garlands of instinct.

Above

the open country.

5.

Roots in soil of dream
branch and shoot   leave time and life
to themselves the abiding present.
And for increase draw sap
in crowning the hilltop late afternoon.
Distant ranges conspicuous
no screening to shroud.

Primateria
whisper wisteria.
Charmed and crossed over.
Widening into view.

6.

The story goes on to tell
the lie of the land
laws of beauty formalized upon a body
awakening.
Smiling to boot
a lower lip running from corners
and this line fastened behind the ear.
Own underneath.

All sorts together with five in seven
four and three
the harmony.

Precisely.
The horizon multiple.

WHOLE SAILING

Greeting The Downpour

A sacrifice in crossing sustained me
brought over the mountain   the back step
finishing touch to an audible snowy drift.
Having kept company   to say nothing
of the fact   or fantasy
the undulating veil of hand-painted trees
already grey caked mud beginning to run
from the top of the bank.

For fear the rain might start again
hastening the gradual decline of day.

Does suffering end?   Suffering ends.
A signal soon forgotten parting white edge
on the moving lake.
The shore   a lighthouse   and glimmering.

Moonlight seizes the paddle.
Rush for deeper water
then shudder a whispered prayer.

A blessing to enter the rapids.

It breaks down
persuades
ravishes in life and death
such words
two alone
like heavy
c
o
l
u
m
n
s
.

Not Hear . . . Yet

there are instances and
there are instances
long words trickling a flood of rhetoric
a dry vivid dusty and static
clinging to a network
vocabulary

so much and so little to say

of the carrying of the hand to the head
is suggestive

acoustic longing
underscoring some vital spot
anxious through this passage
while paper attracts the black mark

an adjective might be mutual
a candor entirely fresh

told so to speak   detached

migrating all down the line

Articulation

Aiming to spin and trivialize an habitual hoax
some basic desire or ambition
tapping dialogue.
For credibility seems apostle
to liberate home for a story.
Cluster the image quicksands intent.

Doubt threading concentric sideline.
Agony named ecstasy to bewilder
where the last word on paper *really* envisions
        a web
of unbroken pattern.

To foresee a telling procession of animated figures.
To hear allegiance recited in unison
      strange and understanding.
To catalogue a single title whose nuance
dies in translation.
A promise in the handbook attend to these.
The real wonder of sweet butter.

And Shine Alike

Tell us what is good as well as bad.
What is genuinely devoted to the many
        and arbitrary.
In subtle incantation
intoxicate or terrify
        or both.
Aversion to reality
anarchy and you're afraid.

Think twice of identical twins
identical thought caught
trespassing.

This height   that peach
this account a sequence growing pale.
Slow habits in slow motion.
The ground roars provocation.
Preferred lavender.   And courage.

What will be uncovered
and the sorting to restore.
        Mind over mind.
        Matter under matter.
In half-light a listening
with only half-attention.
Chair and lamp casting spells
within everyday use.

Residue The Probe

Half turned toward it   exposed to enter in
approach softened a deep furrow
so that it shone   seafaring
into fine diagonal folds.

For the balsams in truth anoint
and duration stands quite near
so that we sit down and bargain.

> I will give you writing   paper
> without conditions   without price
> but weight in powdery
> ochre.

Translate as you stand
roll and ready.
This falling star recited aloud
and a rain of sparks in the strengthened white.

What people are those?
Question the asking an odd sensation.
Recognize and turn now
for I've said it twice already.
Not without pain in parting.

Showing The Whites

Camel-load of pistachio
all here is there about.
Sweet meat on a fallen quarry
ruminating its practical
                                        (aside).
Kept quiet about it.

Silent consequence of the tight place
unnerving accord the desert custom.
Trail quench of that solitary figure
secure in absence.
Perfectly calm and recomposed.

Hold them with whom   to and fro among
the children their mouths bolt upright.
One in the other license of tongue
shedding allegory.

But let that pass.

Flourish of speech be jesting.
The large lines laid down
incline a deep breath back to its source.
What say?   Words.
Worlds a part
suiting actions to strands of pearls.

Hence My Pallor

Four days nimble in separate dwellings
saddle and tent mediate syntax
cinnamon beneath a threshold
and what is passing
    over.
They change places.
Across the board and laid upon a chair
ankle-length with sleeves
sit here.

Formal and oblique clothe
feeling in the deepest sense.
A warning held together by slow degrees.

The waning medium swells some short space
some better choice their in.
Free spirit the greening that swarms
a slender bark with citadel
aspiring to the greatest change.

What is the meaning even though familiar
intensely simple yet a guide?

Grounds of higher necessity *happened.*
Sun-warmed all these uncounted days
rolling in a stretch of pressed fruit.
Two or more together converging.
Illusion.   Perspective.
Then find little difference
confusion and a peculiar bliss.
Mud and dignity hand in hand.

Depth Of Field

we can't take leave of all that goes
on
          in the pre-noon hours
tracking a dense mass
itself a current in two directions
drifting so close the tamed lines enterprise
an intimate glimpse of entry

waves roll in
medium of utterance with survey outstretched
one after the other
name precedes named
with unerring instinct
the answer
        overlapping
              the question

subject matters   arbitrary
comes closest to it
followed in cauldron
the depths fulfill
a third dimension in constant flood

In Her Errant Verity

unexpected leaps will be raised
by diverse loves and passions
because of a blackmailer beyond the display
while this sunset is written
windows flashing gold like dandelion

abbreviated by gradual darkening
some vast remoteness hastens the entire cabinet
well before a landscape of rubble

more than anything
more than radical
equal views poise at the brink of extinction
most have come to pass
to conduct parallel along the unexplored
abrasive fable

nestled under tarpaulin
a flush of respect generated by the full moon
slowly reels in a line
and retires for the night

*

only to have it thrown
edged through a grinding mass of perfect chaos
a nearby bluff profusions then peters out

had it been

tropical or filling
lagoon rather than severe drought
it would murmur and still be
heaven scent
chalkbed of memory outcrop

vines and ancient abundance
scale the rapid change seven miles up
to strange twilight
to wilderness so thick it had to be faced
in exact detail
the richness negotiating a minimum of five years
its own revolution an exhaustive round
including correspondence
fear on a desert hillock
an almost complete skeleton

*

birds then circle
some eclipsed in the minds of some
resolution upon the bridge of a dark companion

it is one thing
a crown
and a bunch of keys
single file down the centre
issuing direction
                                        (for the hell of it)

rows upon rows upon rows
flat and open to secrecy

to secrecy in a familiar setting
sun

                    setting

Style

set in low relief
settling from flight in differing
royal simulation rivets natty
while creatures honeysuckle origin
pediments and the early printers

parchments free the climbing tendrils
then reappear subtly to concentrate tapestry
weaving an easy stroke upon the loom
and crafty

bestiaries
their Noahs paired by the lure of mirror
even words
        songs
                ivory the vegetation
first perfume of flowering faculty

far easterns pause to clap blue lightning
scattered before testimony
            nearer than near

dawn surfacing to tile a list
derived from joy and a whole room
beauty sensed within
this sense of beauty
the clearly polished millennia reflect

sweet consort of malachite
                                        mediation of detailed swirl
convoluted
                        forest

Abundance Of Shores

through thick and thin
and flight of association
all eyes and ears let me be
            clear

they already mean three things
heaven a gliding vault
the stage black ink and contradiction
from beginning
                        to end

but we need ideas down here in the audience
some attention to the universal number
jungle flower   slender famine
laughter and weeping
            and furthermore
                                    a journey

first on one leg
then another
still more stirring
into regions beyond borders
of hindsight or circumstance

            to make small into space
            habitual comfort a vexation
            all blossoming difficult
            fragrant   beshadowed

until home is above and below
        bobbing up and down
a screw loose somewhere
securing an accurate reading

Invention Of Early Afternoon

without forfeiting all to keep
the endless gradually presented as these
then   one from two
                                        the living
                                                            the dead
ways of thinking

between them the dream knows
infinity adding less the years
posturing speech with fate floating lotus

notice
the path on treading awakened
gliding through the moment
everything to pomegranate and aura
harbouring in warm oil until the thrilling junipers
green under a moccasin of passing
cloud

two great blue herons

blue carries an image of brilliance
an act of eternal youth
buttressing the inner precinct
of an admiring circle

and morning called young
old as night

Awakening

it was
and that is
a section of backyard
watered and cared for
        watered and cared
someone understands roses

more intricate than surface
an entire life compacted to a touch
becomes a trellis
rotated from the vertical in a new direction

wet feet turning the burning soil
night   white   cotton
its mysteries bridge the doubled answer
            across and across
the wrong right one

perplexity another name for the world
this garden grateful of the thorn
its point to draw within a small circumference
                a finger
                                of revealing fluid
                dripping with untold stillness
                optical
                                and infrared

Soft Ground And Telescopic

sketches in a complex matter
provide relief with the exuberant curve
its borders elusive between these hands
fledging urgency in quiet darkness

cold night sky over glacier
painstaking any warm ability
to penetrate the canopy
and capture the next rim

space
            a sense of measure
a never never end of
                  detail

circling above

            elope
then
            eloquence
or
            else

their slow orbit revolutionary
to what follows or precedes

ruins still standing

Vehicle

a riot of broken surrounded by adhesive
becomes clear
                                        opening to window
night raining the morning of Thursday
showers of amber glow internal
incandescence
          essence of cloud walking upon the earth

by walking
the statement "all chairs have legs"
distributes the term "chair"
the letter couched in burgundy
vowels flaming delivery to define obsidian
as glass

writing becoming
                                        passing
and becoming again
                                        as delta
                                                            designed to shine there
                                                            shrine there

                                                            calm and almost taught
                                                            with curving and purple sail

Witness

stretched between literal and figurative
the noise was heard of two pieces
one for document
one for written descent

(which fell)

the resulting fragments whistling like a smooth lawn
the big light roaring itself through
a ringing issue of ownership
falling from the sky
on property

gravitational

and vaporized

Dextrous Crawl

indefinitely better spirits
did this time high the other way round
to contain it
for it was not yet another hand
and the feelings of one standing
can be elsewise too
    of course

I am disoriented
and jest with mining
countless gems cut brilliant
means with all of us
all passing strange
to shiver and then some
the ceaseless echo complains
    living a repetitive and monotonous life

    living a repetitive and monotonous life

So To Speak

moonlit lowland
riddle a hand-held universe
I tell thee this
I tell thee with numbers the renewal now
and later confuse hot with open
silkily the scarlet rays propel but whistle
but first

the fading glow of many centres
so many better than one gone mad
none in front and not better
three six and besides
triple a clear that will not hear
that is its name
not to know this
not hold and not go together
so curious interrupted
pattern perplexity
dismay yes and alarm encounter
candour obscure uncanny

increase
increase

*

          by the margin it looked
melancholy opposite
the mere thought at the thought of
I heard belly sparkle
and slumbering
          however dawn shaken
chill winds suffuse a parallel route
ravish the blind urge in hair its length
falling visibly nudge and waited

good   very good
well meant by
                  a single mulberry
red and white

clove

pinks

*

according deliberate bearing
we should say the middle
a year and seasons

a new definition
above all a new thing
bounded by equal angles

in structure of place
the first gleam opens a square with gazing
sun-instructed   listened to
and the gift of days
born without saying
hours a constellation
hypothetical bases drawn through

tarum-tum   tarum

embrace and kiss
apex
farther down   or up
into the smooth clay
still lay
oscillations

*

submerge and mirror the soft swoop
the picture of men and things
for instance

to sound like metal
difference rings out harshly
and distance proffers a narrowing platform

eye to eye on one leg
in one hand
how shall I
(amazed from the holding up)
recognize the likeness
lifting
brow

*

transcribe to this the same image
one moment imitation and
succession

pattern the impress now speaks of itself
it tells
                of the years
in a word
                long since
divine
                in a line

not only that it was divided
     the true and the actual
but as though a voice had got
to its feet

*

for neither lacking in view from will
influence could easily lead one

                                        a stray of misgivings
to come over trembling a neither-nor
as it was
too complicated and kindly

and now details occupy as gardener
not of course burnt and hung
not only forester
but bunches of all sorts
fructifying pollen on a steady head of padded rope

partly to relieve fading
they look at the same
vista lower still
height instead of leaving to call it so

were they numerous
the stages after twelve?
because it is both incredulous and eloquent
    grove here
instead of turning back

instead of not badly

*

how prosperity smiles after midday
moving carefully as though glass
noting the shadow on the clock
transparent   (tucked in a little)
the floor a design of heaven
and by the door

meanwhile passes through and finds
a path of lime to a full basin
    on that green reflection swim surroundings
    so lifelike that one kneels down
    in black and white

*

that might be let and hasten
in the full sense of the word for word
for mutual and the odd form
where it is cool and a school of thought
may read a clear idea to rival
this being
the custom lip and moist
issued out among the orchards
first and always after
climber of trees astride the canal
full to overflowing mother   tongue
inlaid with stone and variable currents
water poured over giving back the light

sky-blue beams

gazelle

*

so now
when free and apprentice average for reason
the sum looking calm
fed from the same source
out of carelessness   or worse
and these large and fierce
    disturbing
equivocal sensations alongside
the sequel endless and uniform
won over in the same wise
    disguise
the fact that one's eyes
reach the ear
and gladden

*

engendered
but not yet risen
sun and shoulders above a case in
sight and sound long since
scattered to the four

while solitary considered beneath a moon of numbers
moon rising noon spring fertility
overleaping the nearest hanging